Christmas Ukulele
Hawaiian Style

Play Christmas Ukulele Hawaiian Style with ukulele
expert Chika Nagata. Included in this book/CD are 12
songs, each played 3 times: the first and third time with
the melody, the second time with the melody left out for
you to play or sing with just the rhythm.

Cover Art - Eddie Young, thanks Eddie
Cover Design - Eric Peterson
Layout - David Collins

ISBN-13: 978-1-57424-207-2
ISBN-10: 1-57424-207-5
SAN-683-8022

© 2006 Centerstream Publication LLC.
P.O. Box 17878 - Anaheim Hills, CA 92817
All rights for publication and distribution are reserved.

Contents & CD Track List

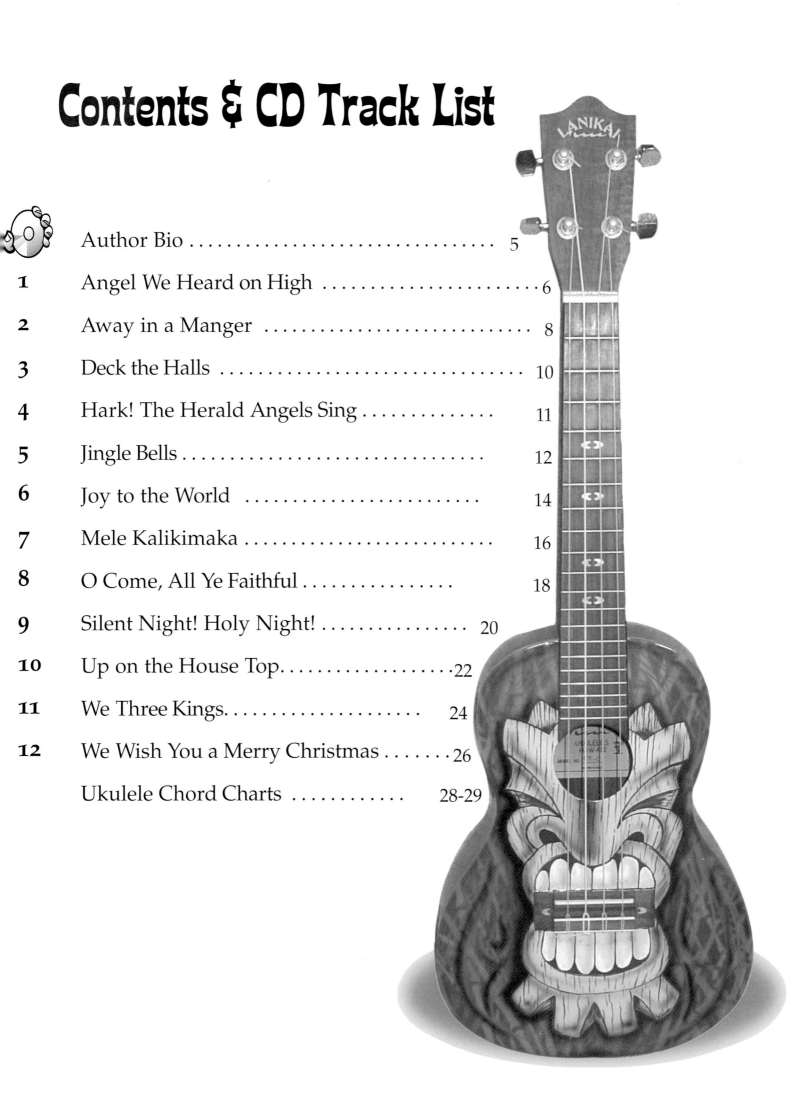

Authors

Chika Nagata

My love of music started around the age nine when I received my first ukulele for about $5.00 in the late 1940's. I've played for many years professionally and started teaching fundamentials of ukulele music. I now enjoy teaching several ukulele classes in the Los Angeles, South Bay area. I also entertain with various professionally music groups performing at several Hawaiian events and backyard parties. I play and record on an eight string ukulele.

Randall Ames

Randall Ames is a composer/arranger residing in southern California where he owns and operates a digital recording studio. It is there where he constructs his works of art from the initial inception to the finished product. Randall's credits include arrangements of numerous culturally diverse songs and arrangements for symphonic band and orchestra.

Angels We Have Heard On High

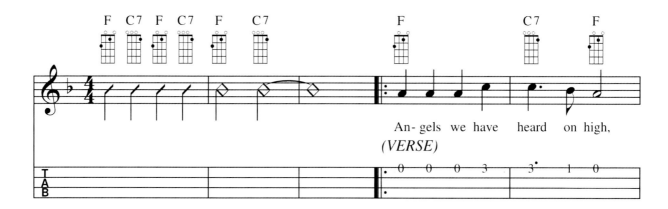

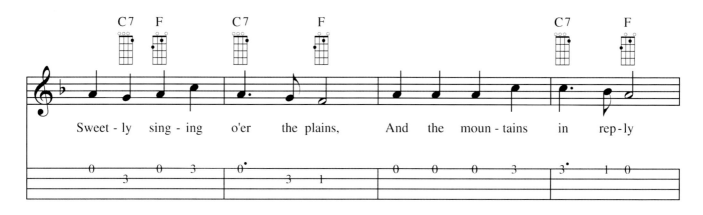

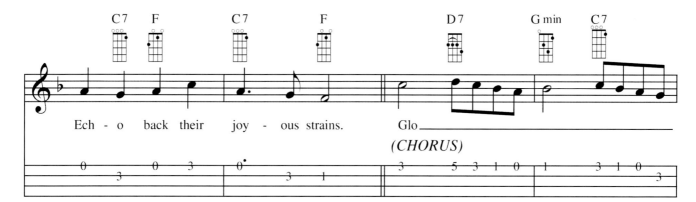

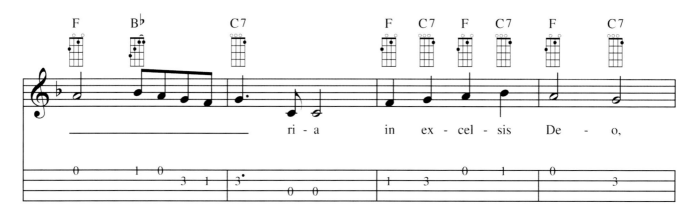

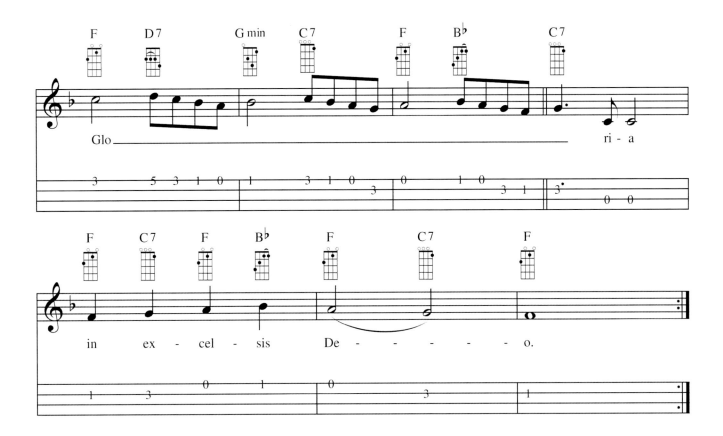

Glo _____ ri - a

in - ex - cel - sis De - - - - o.

Early 1940's Hawaiian backyard party

Away in a Manger

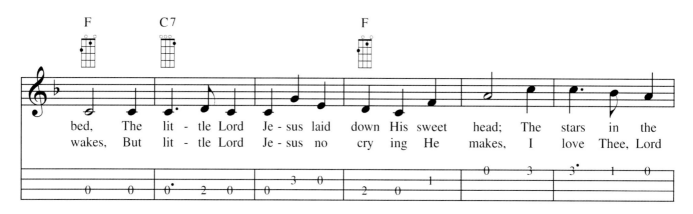

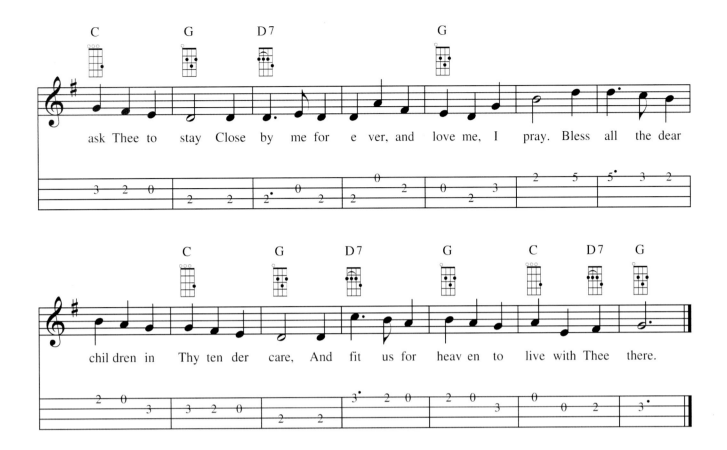

ask Thee to stay Close by me for e ver, and love me, I pray. Bless all the dear

chil dren in Thy ten der care, And fit us for heav en to live with Thee there.

Riding the Longboards out beyond the Corral Reef at Waikiki, circa 1940.

Deck the Halls

Hark! the Herald Angels Sing

Jingle Bells

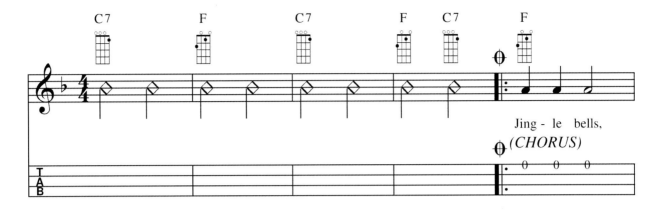

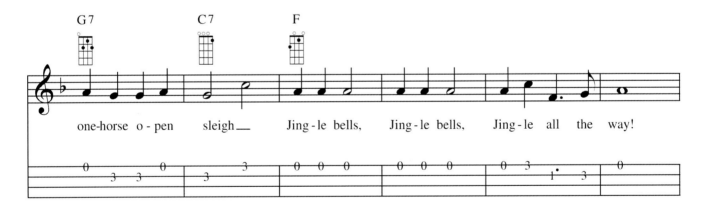

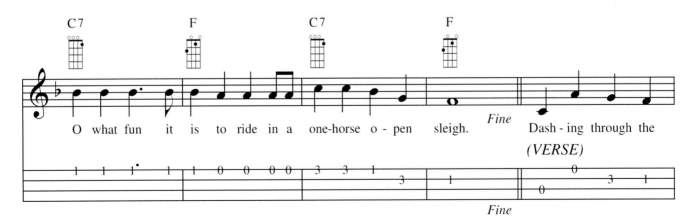

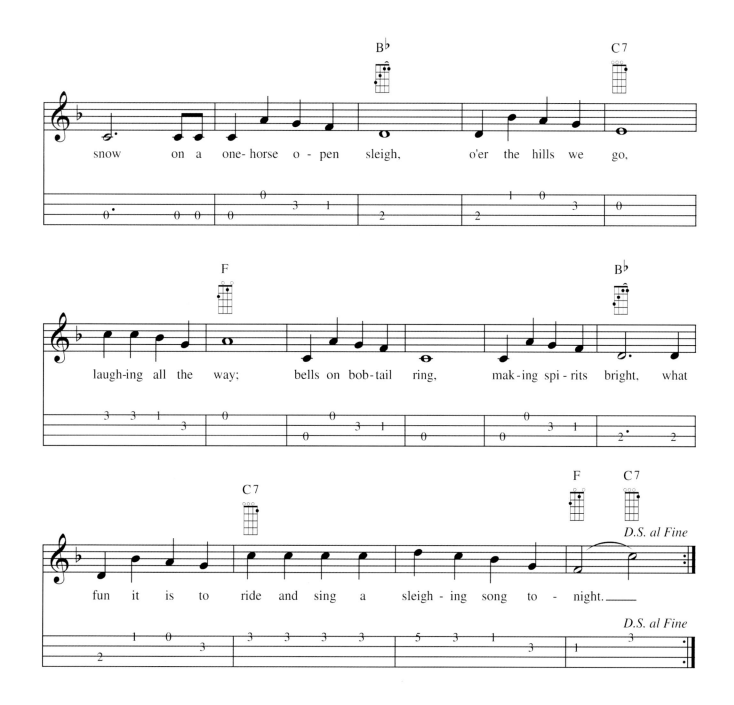

snow on a one-horse o - pen sleigh, o'er the hills we go,

laugh-ing all the way; bells on bob-tail ring, mak-ing spi - rits bright, what

D.S. al Fine

fun it is to ride and sing a sleigh - ing song to - night.____

D.S. al Fine

Early Hawaiian hula dancers.

13

Joy to the World

Early Hawaiian promotional brochure.

Mele Kalikimaka

Words and Music by Alex Anderson

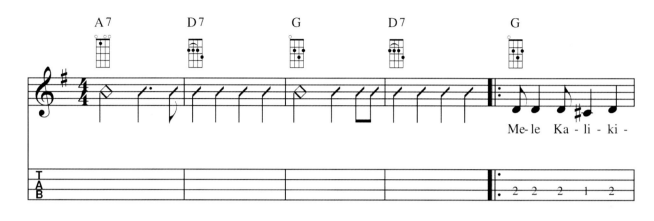

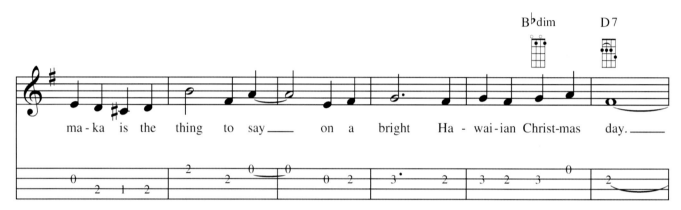

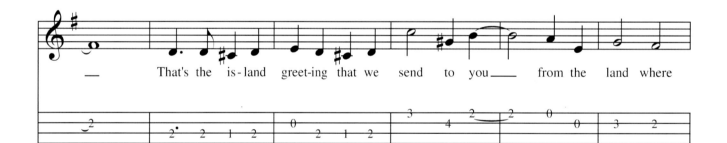

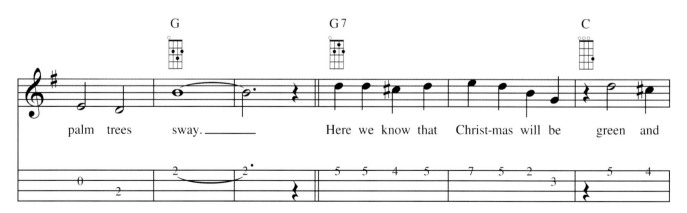

bright. The sun will shine by day and all the stars at night. Me-le-Ka li-ki-ma-ka is Ha-

wai-i's way to say Mer-ry Christ-mas! to you. _____

O Come, All Ye Faithful

Hawaiian Performing Troup

Silent Night! , Holy Night!

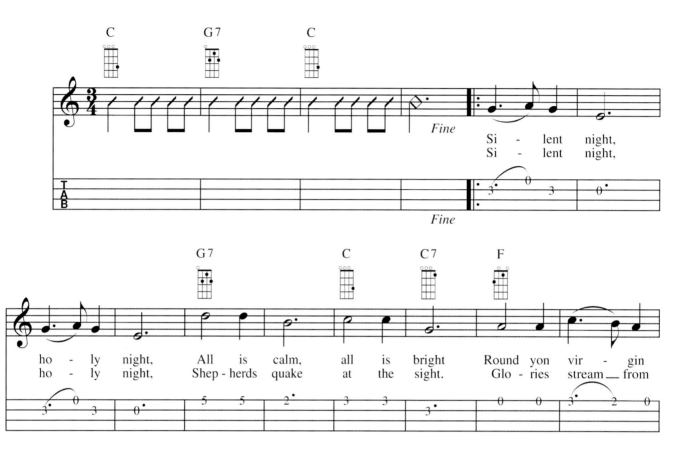

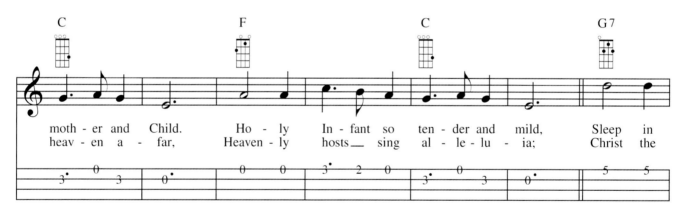

Up on the Housetop

MikiLan'i Fo, Steel Guitarist and all around instrumentalist and entertainer, 1953.

We Three Kings

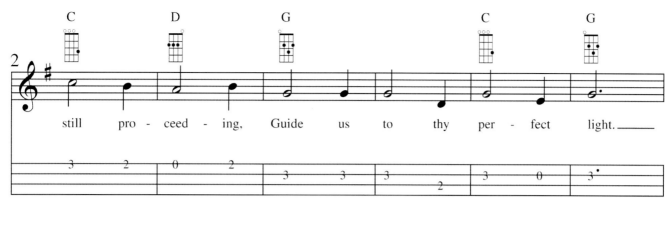

still pro - ceed - ing, Guide us to thy per - fect light._____

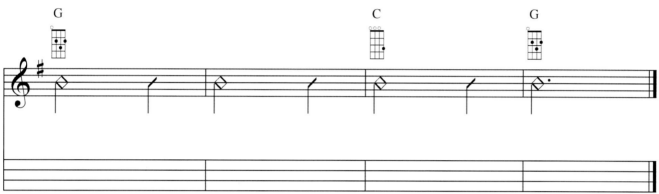

Dancers and musicians, early 1940's postcard.

We Wish You a Merry Christmas

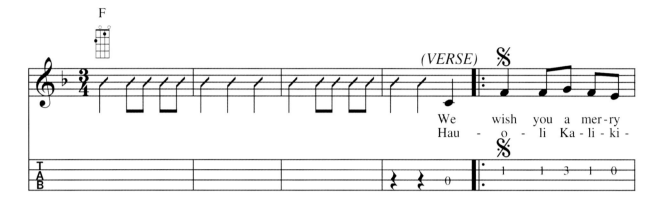

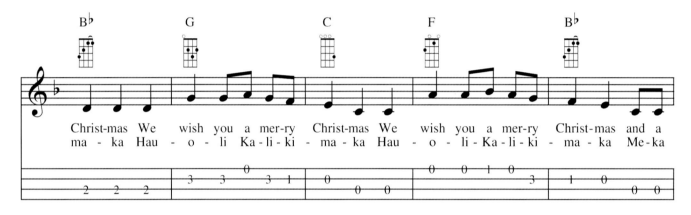

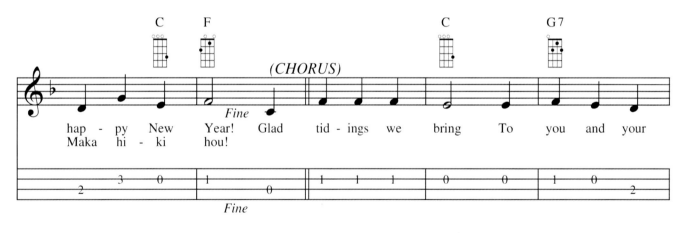

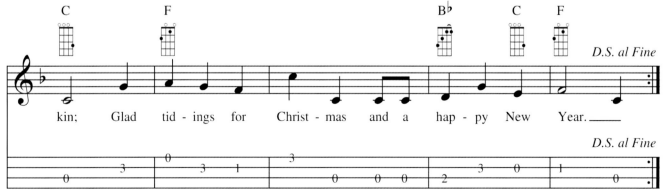

© Centerbrook

```
  4 3 2 1
  G C E A
```
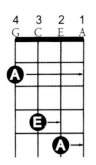

Relative Tuning

Whenever a pitch pipe, piano or another tuned ukulele is not available to you for tuning, the relative tuning method can be used. This method will allow the uke to be in tune with itself, but not necessarily in tune with any other instrument.

1. Turn the tuning peg of the 1st string (A) until it is fairly tight and produces a high tone.
2. Press the 5th fret of the 2nd string (E) and tune to <u>equal</u> the pitch of the 1st string (A).
3. Press the 4th fret of the 3rd string (C) and tune to <u>equal</u> the pitch of the 2nd string (E).
4. Press the 2nd fret of the 4th string (G) and tune to <u>equal</u> the pitch of the 1st string (A).

Ukulele Fingerboard

If you see the sharp symbol #, it means to *raise* the pitch one fret higher. The flat symbol b means to *lower* the pitch one fret back.

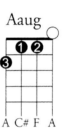

1st string
2nd string
3rd string
4th string

Ukulele Chords

The chord fingerings are only suggestive, you may find other fingerings that are easier.

A	A7	Am	Am7	Adim	Aaug	A9
A C# E A	G C# E A	A C E A	G C E A	A D# F# C	A C# F A	G C# E B

A# same as Bb

Bb	Bb7	Bbm	Bbm7	Bbdim	Bbaug	Bb9
Bb D F Bb	Ab D F Bb	Bb Db F Bb	Ab Db F Bb	G Db E Bb	Bb D F# Bb	Ab D F C

B	B7	Bm	Bm7	Bdim	Baug	B9
B D# F# B	B D# F# A	B D F# B	A D F# B	G# D F B	B D# G B	A D# F# C#

C	C7	Cm	Cm7	Cdim	Caug	C9
G C E C	G C E Bb	G Eb G C	Bb Eb G C	A Eb Gb C	G# C E C	G D E Bb

C# same as Db

Db	Db7	Dbm	Dbm7	Dbdim	Dbaug	Db9
Ab Db F Db	Ab Db F B	B D Gb B	B E Ab Db	G Db E Bb	A Db F A	Ab Eb F B

28

D — A D F# A
D7 — A D F# C
Dm — A D F A
Dm7 — C F A D
Ddim — G# D F B
Daug — A# D F# A#
D9 — A E F# C

D# same as Eb

Eb — G Eb G Bb
Eb7 — Bb Eb G Db
Ebm — Bb Eb Gb Bb
Ebm7 — Bb Eb Gb Db
Ebdim — A Eb Gb C
Ebaug — B Eb G B
Eb9 — G Db F Bb

E — B E G# B
E7 — G# D F B
Em — G E G B
Em7 — B E G D
Edim — G C# E A#
Eaug — G# C E C
E9 — G# D F# B

F — A C F A
F7 — A Eb F A
Fm — Ab C F C
Fm7 — Ab Eb F C
Fdim — G# D F B
Faug — A C# F A
F9 — A Eb G C

F# same as Gb

Gb — Bb Db Gb Bb
Gb7 — Bb E Gb Db
Gbm — A Db Gb A
Gbm7 — A E Gb Db
Gbdim — A Eb Gb C
Gbaug — Bb D Gb Bb
Gb9 — Ab Db E Bb

G — G D G B
G7 — G D F B
Gm — G D G Bb
Gm7 — G D F Bb
Gdim — G C# E Bb
Gaug — B D# G B
G9 — A D F B

G# same as Ab

Ab — C Eb Ab C
Ab7 — Ab Eb Gb C
Abm — B Eb Ab B
Abm7 — Ab Eb Gb B
Abdim — Ab D F B
Abaug — Ab C E C
Ab9 — Bb Eb Gb C

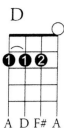

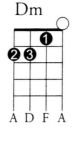
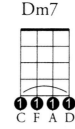

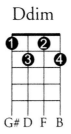
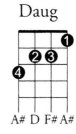
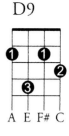
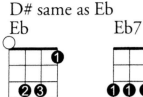
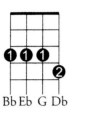

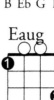
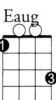

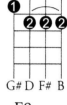

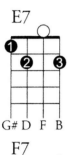
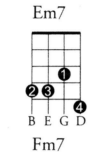
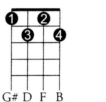
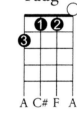

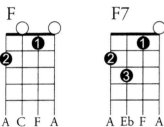

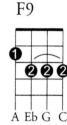
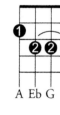
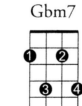

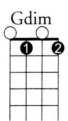

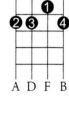
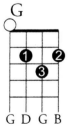
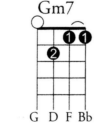
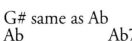
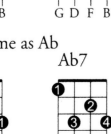
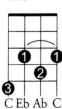

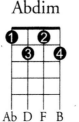
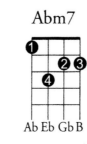

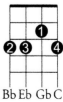

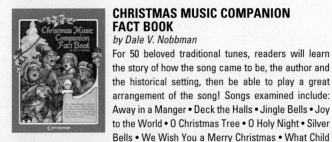

Those using
Centerstream
Books & DVDs

The Competition